The Four Falling Seasons

Kayvonna Tolbert-Stigall

The Four Falling Seasons
Copyright © 2019 Kayvonna Stigall

All rights reserved. All rights reserved. No part of this book may be copied or reproduced in any form without written permission from the publisher.

Illustrations: Mayaria Williams

ISBN: 978-1-937400-98-9

Printed in the United States of America

PeeWee Press, A Division of Manifold Grace Publishing House, LLC
Southfield, Michigan 48033
www.manifoldgracepublishinghouse.com

Dedicated to Karvon and Kayla

Fall

Crisp leaves falling like a melody playing, while the trees sway surrenders to the days rested wind

Fall

In Fall the leaves are falling

making pictures on the ground

Red, yellow, orange,green

and some are turning brown.

The wind is sometimes so confused

it flows around about.

The sun is really curious

So it goes in and out.

Winter

Soft flakes falling like a ballerina dancing while branches lay nestled under a blanket of snow

Winter

In Winter falls the snow so cold

yet warming to the eye.

The snowflakes all so different shaped

And unique like you and I!

Spring

Rain drops falling like a traffic light blinking while colors run while on the grass and trees

Spring

In Spring falls rain that brings all new,

the flowers from their sleep.

The birds, the bees, fun living things

Oh, how it's such a treat!

Summer

Sunshine falling like a warm kissed muffin on the break of a beautiful fun-filled day!

Summer

In Summer falls the warm sun rays

with a flow so shiny bright

Oh how summer brings hot happy days

with cool, calm, collective nights!

My Love for the Four Falling Seasons

Fall
The Fall time brings colorful leaves
Pumpkin smiles
And all warm things
I love the smell of apple cider
And warm donuts, oh what a treat!

Winter
The winter time brings glistening snowflakes
Cozy coats and boots
I love the smell of hot chocolate
And warm chocolate chip cookies, oh what a treat!

Spring
The Spring time brings rainbow rainy days
Dancing in a circle of colorful flowers
I love the smell of blueberries in a bowl
And a cool cup of pudding, oh what a treat!

Summer
The Summer time brings rainbow sun-filled days
Splashing pool fun
And longer days
I love the smell of fresh lemonade
And a cool grape popsicle, oh what a treat!

Author

Kayvonna Tolbert-Stigall is a native of River Rouge, Michigan. She is married and has two children. She enjoys writing poetry, short stories and spending time with her family. Mrs. Stigall spent over 15 years as an early childhood educator. She has published two collections of inspirational poetry and looks forward to continuing to share her love of poetry and writing with others! She also enjoys hosting poetry events and teaching creative writing to children and young adults. Kayvonna Stigall is the owner of *I Spit Ink*, her poetry hosting event arm.

May, our illustrator, is 11 years old and is from Lakeland, Florida.

Mrs. Stigall can be reached via:
Email: info@riseaboveclouds.com
Website: www.riseaboveclouds.com

www.ingramcontent.com/pod-product-compliance
Lightning Source LLC
Chambersburg PA
CBHW051404110526
44592CB00023B/2953